How to Make Manga Characters

Written and illustrated
by Katy Coope

Contents

Collins

What is manga?

Manga is a Japanese word and it originally meant something like "pictures for entertainment". Today in Japan it means "comics" – and it is the word we use for a special style of comic, which once came from Japan but which now can come from almost anywhere in the world.

Manga developed first in Japan and it soon became very popular, perhaps because there are manga comics for everyone. There are manga aimed specially at boys, at girls, at children and adults.

There are many different kinds of manga stories, from crazy comedies and exciting adventures, to beautiful romances and serious dramas.

Manga is drawn and published very quickly and in Japan, episodes of manga stories come out every week, bound up together in huge books. The most popular stories are then collected into books of their own. Many are translated into other languages and sent to book and comic shops all round the world.

The Japanese language is read from right-to-left, instead of left-to-right like English, so a Japanese manga book begins on what would – in an English book – be the last page. To make it easier, some translators flip the artwork around. But some leave it "back-to-front", so that you can see it exactly as it was drawn. In this book, I have drawn the manga pages to be read in the English way.

Manga is usually drawn in black and white for speed, but the characters will often be in colour on the cover. Special pages of a story may also be in colour.

This comic reads right-to-left, like a Japanese comic. Here's a key to help you read it in the right order.

Key

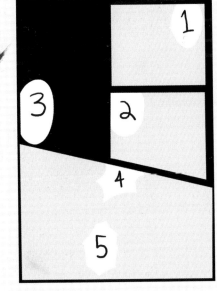

What is anime?

Japanese animation is called anime (pronounced *an–e–may*). There are many kinds of anime. Some are set in real life, some are fantasy or science fiction. Often anime are based on manga or video games. They are aimed at adults as well as children. In many countries, they became popular even before manga comics.

How did manga begin?

Manga can be traced back to traditional Japanese art, but manga as we know it today came to life in the 1950s, after the Second World War. One of the first well-known manga artists – or mangaka – was Osamu Tezuka, and some of his characters, like Astroboy, are still popular.

A lot of early manga was inspired by the cute and cool characters of American cartoons, but over time manga and anime creators have made it into something new.

Who makes manga?

While most manga is drawn by the Japanese, there are people everywhere who love drawing it too. One of the interesting things about manga is that it uses stories from all over the world, old and new.

This book will tell you about making manga characters yourself, so you can make manga comics of your own.

Hi there! I'm Ayako-chan! I'm here to give you tips and show you around the world of manga.

What makes manga special?

Manga is special in many ways. It's aimed at everyone, boys and girls, children and adults. It also has:

- all kinds of stories – adventure, sport, real life, science fiction, fantasy, mystery

- action-filled plots and crazy humour

- **stylised** characters, often with pointed **features** and larger than average heads, huge eyes and wild hair

- wild and wonderful creatures and animals

- powerful and adventurous children

- **underdog** characters who often succeed against unbelievable odds.

Today, manga is also published on the web and in Japan, there are even cafés where you can sit and read the latest manga comics over your favourite soft drink.

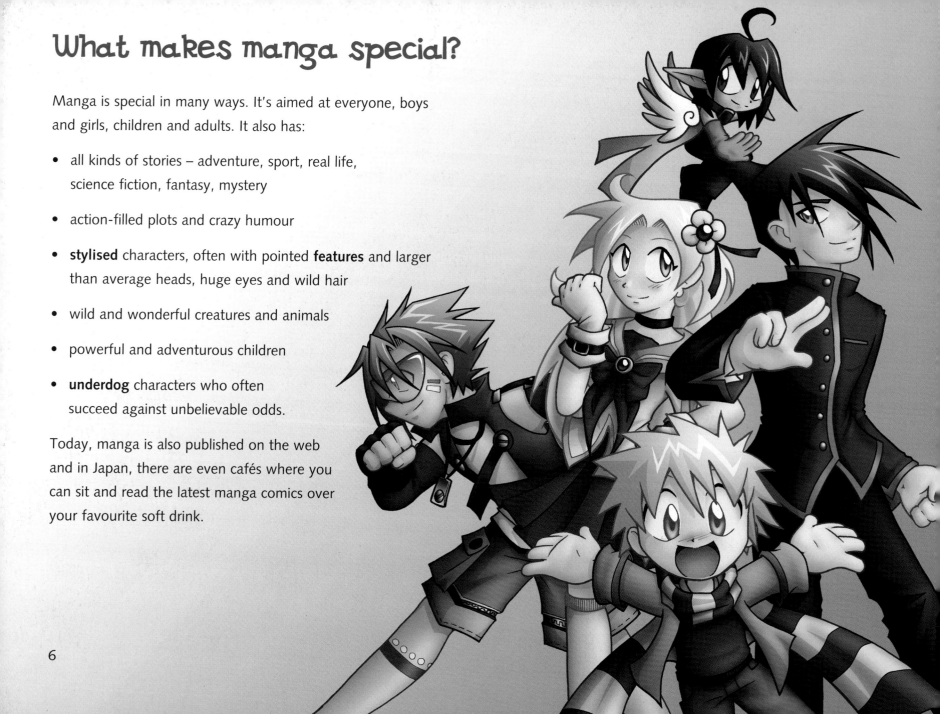

How to start: materials

To start drawing manga you need paper, pencils and a rubber.

In this book you will see how to begin by drawing your character in pencil. Then you can go over the lines in ink and rub out the pencil lines. Afterwards, you can add colour, if you like.

Manga characters are usually drawn by hand, but today, many artists also use computers to help them. With a little experience, you can do this too.

You also need your own ideas, and that's the fun part!

coloured inks, paints, pens and pencils

Pens:
Use a medium pen to start with and a thin one for details.

Rubber:
Use a good quality rubber.

Paper:
A sketchbook will keep your drawings safely together.

Pencils:
"HB" pencils are good. "B" pencils are darker but they can smudge.

The basics: drawing a manga head

Now you are ready to grab a pencil and start drawing.

The most important part of a character is the head, so this is where we'll begin.

The best way to start is to break down what you are drawing into simple shapes. One of the most important shapes is the ball, or **sphere**. You can start all your characters' heads in the same way, even if they end up looking different.

Step 1

- Draw a sphere.
- Now draw a curve for the chin.

Notice that the chin line crosses the sphere about two thirds of the way round.

$\frac{1}{3}$ $\frac{1}{3}$ $\frac{1}{3}$

Step 2

- Draw guidelines to work out where the features – the eyes, mouth and nose – should be. First draw three eye guidelines. The middle one comes halfway down the face. Finally, draw a guideline from the top of the head to the chin to show where the nose will go.

This line is halfway down the face.

$\frac{1}{2}$

$\frac{1}{2}$

Press lightly with your pencil!

Key

1
2 } eye guidelines
3

4   nose guideline

This face is looking to the side, so the nose guideline is over to the side, too.

Step 3

- Above the end of the chin curve, draw a C for the ear.
- Now you can begin to shape the face. Using the eye guidelines, cut a curve out of the side of the face.
- Add in a couple of lines for the neck.

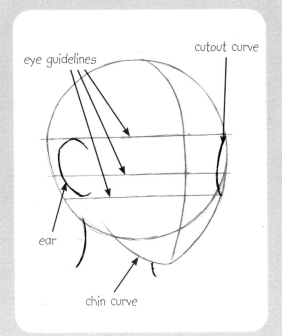

eye guidelines

cutout curve

ear

chin curve

Step 4

- Now draw the eyes. Draw a pair of curves going up to the top eye line.
- Underneath the two top curves, add a pair of smaller curves on the bottom eye line.
- Next draw an oval shape for one **iris** and then another for the other iris.

The eye that is further away from us is a little smaller.

iris

The curve starts near the middle eye line and goes up to the top eye line.

Step 5

- Draw a **pupil** inside each iris.
- Now put in the highlight. This is a little oval shape near the top of each iris and it will make your eye look shiny.
- Finally, draw a pair of curves above the eyes for the eyebrows.

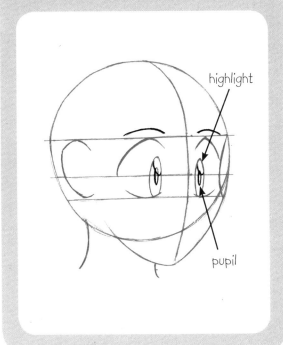

highlight

pupil

Your face is beginning to come to life. If you make a mistake, don't worry. You can always rub out the line and try again if you draw lightly.

Step 6

- Draw a tilted tick shape for the nose.
- About halfway between the nose and the bottom of the chin, draw a curve for the mouth.

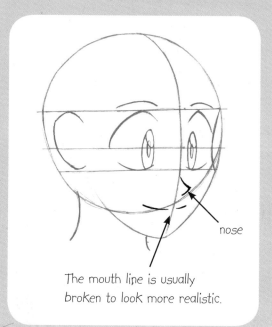

nose

The mouth line is usually broken to look more realistic.

Step 7

Now give your character some hair. You can make it as wild as you like.

- Draw some pointed curves around the top and side of your character's head. Add some more across the forehead to make a fringe.

The more you draw, the easier it gets!

Step 8

Nearly there! Time to add the final details.

- Add some curves inside the ear.
- Draw a little line under the mouth to make a bottom lip.
- You can also put a couple of "blush" lines at the top of the cheeks.

Now you've finished your pencil drawing.

Step 9

- Next, go over the lines you want to keep in ink. Experiment with different pens to find one that suits you.

- At last, you can rub out all the pencil lines! But take care that the ink is dry, or it will smudge.

Step 10

- Now you can colour in your face with pencils, paint or coloured pens.

You've finished your first manga face!

Drawing manga eyes

Let's take a look at different ways of drawing the eyes. Manga eyes come in lots of shapes, just as real ones do, but you don't need to draw all the lines of the shape, every time. There are five main parts to manga eyes.

1 Shape

Here, I've left out some of the lines in the middle and at the side of the eye.

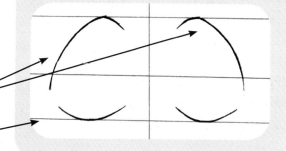

We are looking at the eyes from the front, so they are both the same.

eye guideline

2 Eyelids

The eyelids follow the shape of the eye. The top lid is usually heavier and darker.

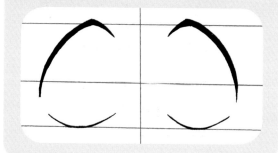

3 Iris

This can be an oval or a circle, big or small. Part of it can be covered by the upper or lower eyelid.

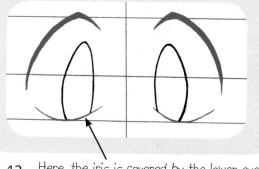

Here, the iris is covered by the lower eyelid.

4 Pupil

This is the same shape as the iris and can be big or small. There is a highlight on the iris to make it look shiny, like a real eye.

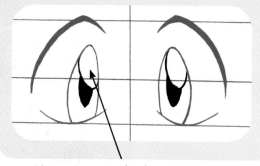

Manga eyes nearly always have a highlight.

5 Eyebrows

These are important for showing **expressions**. I have used gently curved ones here.

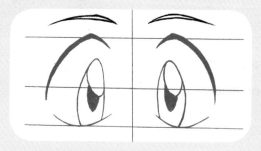

Here are some more eyes.

Try experimenting with drawing eyes in different ways.

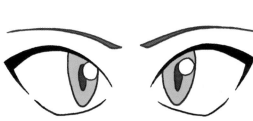

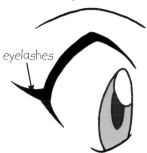
eyelashes

This eye is oval-shaped with points at the ends. Narrow eyes can make a character look suspicious or unfriendly.

Big eyes can make a character look attractive and approachable. This character has thick eyelashes and is a girl.

Try covering the top of the iris with an eyelid. This can make your character look tired.

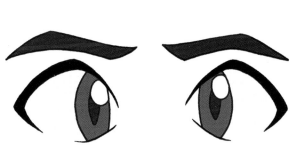

Thick eyebrows can make a character look older.

These characters have very different personalities. Can you tell this from their eyes?

Drawing manga hair

Manga characters are known for their wild and crazy hair styles. Drawing manga hair looks complicated at first, but you can break it down into easy shapes, just as you did with the face. Most manga hair is made from a collection of curved and pointed shapes. The points should always come at the ends of the hair.

You can collect these together to make bigger or more interesting shapes.

To add hair to your character, draw the shapes you have chosen around the top of the head, then add some to the sides. You could also draw some covering the face at the front.

Manga hair comes in all the colours of the rainbow!

14

Hair can give you clues about a character and show what a person is like and how they are feeling. Here are some more tips and ideas to help you draw manga hair.

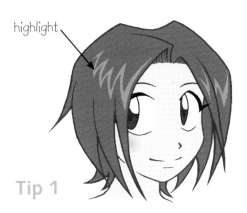

highlight

Tip 1

To make hair look shiny, add a lighter coloured zigzag across it when you colour it in.

Tip 2

Put shapes together with the points going in different directions to make bunches. Short or tied back hair can look great on **energetic** characters.

Tip 3

Hair that hangs over the face or covers one eye can look moody or mysterious.

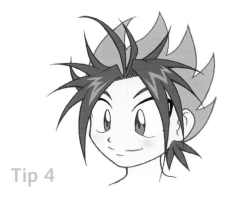

Tip 4

Manga hair doesn't always obey gravity. You can create all kinds of wild and crazy styles!

Tip 5

Even when a character is standing still, if their hair is blowing in the wind it can make a picture look lively and exciting.

Manga masterclass 1: different faces

Now you have mastered drawing the basic face, try drawing faces from different angles. It's simple once you know how.

This is my best side!

Faces from the front

Drawing a face from the front is very similar to drawing a face looking slightly to the side. The difference is that the face is symmetrical – it is the same on each side. Start with a sphere and guidelines. Add a symmetrical curve for the chin.

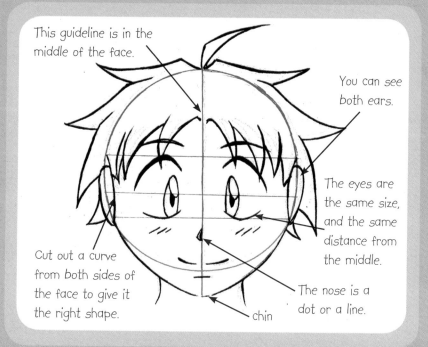

This guideline is in the middle of the face.

You can see both ears.

The eyes are the same size, and the same distance from the middle.

Cut out a curve from both sides of the face to give it the right shape.

chin

The nose is a dot or a line.

Faces from the side

Now try drawing a side view of a face.

Step 1

Begin by drawing a sphere. Next, draw a curve for the chin. Notice that the chin curve is slightly different from before. Remember to draw very lightly at this stage.

Now draw in eye guidelines, as before.

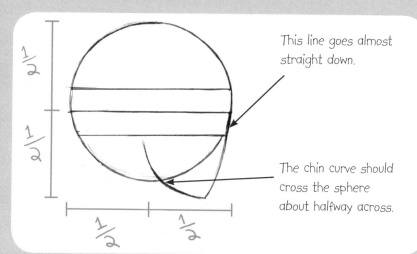

$\frac{1}{2}$

$\frac{1}{2}$

$\frac{1}{2}$

$\frac{1}{2}$

This line goes almost straight down.

The chin curve should cross the sphere about halfway across.

Step 2

Draw the neck and the C shape for an ear. Now draw the eye and a little curve or "cutout" to give the face shape.

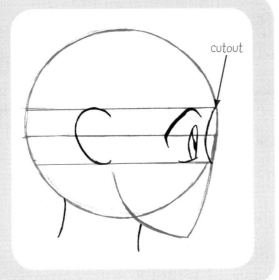

cutout

Step 3

You are now going to draw the nose. Make the "cutout" curve line a little longer, and then draw a line back to the point of the chin, as you can see.

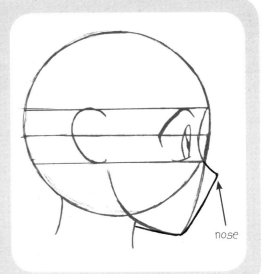

nose

Step 4

Finish the rest of the face as before, by adding eyebrow, mouth, hair and ear detail.

Step 5

Go over the lines in ink, rub out the pencil lines and then add colour. Only ink in the lines you want to keep.

Making your own character

Creating a manga character is really fun. First of all, you need to know what kind of person they are. Then you can decide what they will look like. To do this, you can ask yourself questions about them. It helps if you write the answers down.

- Are they a boy or a girl?
- How old are they?
- Do they have any skills or special powers?
- Where do they live?

Now ask yourself questions about their personality.

- Are they usually cheerful or grumpy?
- Are they brave or cowardly?
- Are they kind and generous, or selfish and mean?
- Can you trust them?
- Do they show how they feel, or do they keep it hidden?
- Do they care about how they look?
- What do they like?
- What don't they like?

If you have any other ideas about your character, write them down, too.

Now you know more about your character, you can think about what they might do and how they might behave. You can ask "what if?" questions.

For example, what if your character found a monster in their garden?

Would they try to fight it?   Or would they run away?   Or would they do something else entirely?

Ask yourself questions like this and you will get a very clear idea about your character.
Here are some more questions to think about. Try writing down some answers.

- What if they found an incredible treasure?
- What if they found out a secret?
- What if they got lost somewhere scary?

- What if they saw somebody in trouble?
- What if their best friend was moving in next door?
- What if they met someone famous?

Making the characters in this book

Just as you doodled with ideas about how your characters behave, you can draw doodles of how they look.

A manga artist will often draw lots of faces before finding the one that looks right. This is how Ayako-chan was created:

Step 1

I started with a basic face shape.

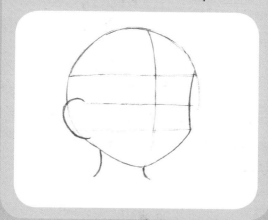

Step 2

Next, I added the features.

I wanted this character to be a girl, so I gave her long eyelashes.

Step 3

Next I added the hair. Short hair suits her because she's active. She cares about how she looks, so some of her hair is tied up.

Step 4

Don't be afraid to change your mind. I always work lightly so I can rub things out.

I changed her eyes to make them less narrow. This makes her look friendlier.

I created these characters to give you some ideas. They live in another world.

Step 5

Finally I picked colours for my character. I wanted her to look unusual so I gave her light blue hair. I wasn't sure if her eyes should be green or purple, but decided green would look best.

Makoto

Makoto is a boy with special powers. He is kind but he can sometimes be a little shy.

Kimi

Kimi is easy-going and friendly. She is brave and quick to act when her friends are in trouble, even when it's dangerous.

Yamato

Yamato also has special powers, but he uses them selfishly. He is proud and cruel to people weaker than he is.

Maru

Maru is a tiny monster but Yamato uses his powers to let him turn into a boy. He is **mischievous** and a bit of a coward.

A change of mood

A character's expression tells you a lot about their personality. Look at these drawings. You can show different expressions by changing eyebrows, eyes or mouth.

Happy

Make the eyebrows a gentle curve a little way above the eyes.

The mouth should be a small curve with the ends pointing upwards.

Gleeful

High eyebrows and big, wide eyes make a character look **gleeful**.

Draw a big smile like a sideways capital letter D.

Unhappy

Curving the eyebrows up in the middle of the face makes someone look unhappy.

Draw eyes half closed or add tears to make them even sadder.

The ends of an unhappy mouth point down.

Angry

Draw eyebrows that point down in the middle of the face.

Eyebrows that cover part of the eye make a character look really cross.

An open mouth shows the character is shouting.

Shocked

Very high eyebrows make a person look surprised.

Wide eyes with small irises and pupils make a person look shocked.

A surprised mouth is rounded.

Mischievous

Looking to the side makes a character look sneaky.

Draw one angry eyebrow and the other raised to show that someone is up to no good.

A smirk is a smile that only curves up at one side.

Eek! It looks like these two disagree about something. What's going to happen?

23

Coming to life

It's time to give your characters bodies! This is not nearly as difficult as it sounds, especially if you use stick people.

First of all, start by drawing a stick figure. This will help you get everything in the right place. It's called getting the **proportions** of your character correct.

Add joints, so that you can see how your stick person could move. A stick figure will help you to try out drawing different ways of standing and moving. These different positions are called "poses".

Draw lots of stick figures in different poses.

Look at all the details on this stick figure!

shoulder

elbow

hip

wrist

knee

ankle

sitting pose

standing pose

Once you are happy with a pose, you can add simple shapes to the stick figure, to make it look like a real body.

A manga artist doesn't start to add details until he or she is happy with the body shape of a character.

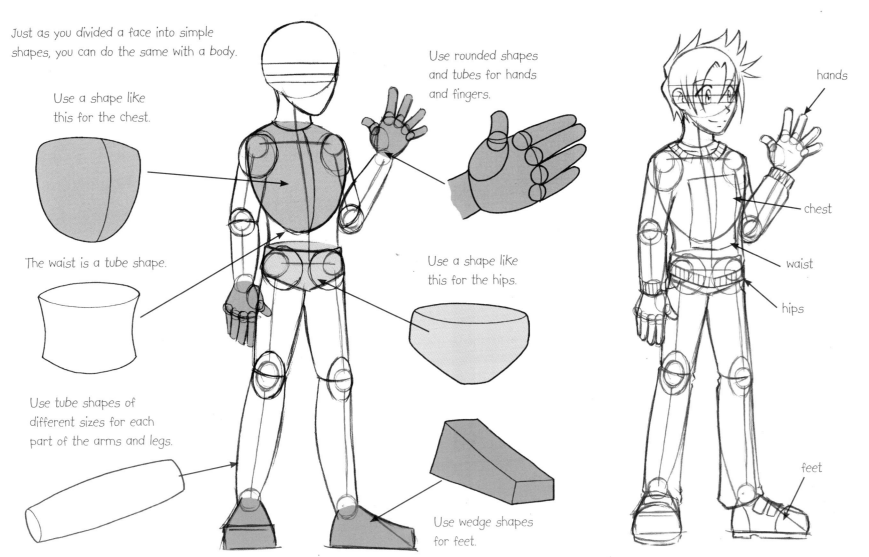

Just as you divided a face into simple shapes, you can do the same with a body.

Use a shape like this for the chest.

The waist is a tube shape.

Use tube shapes of different sizes for each part of the arms and legs.

Use rounded shapes and tubes for hands and fingers.

Use a shape like this for the hips.

Use wedge shapes for feet.

hands

chest

waist

hips

feet

Here are some more tips to help you!

People come in all shapes and sizes, but if you look carefully, you will notice that children have different proportions to adults. Men look different from women. But some proportions are fairly similar in all characters. Have a look at photos of your friends and family, or even pictures in a magazine.

Tip 1

Did you know that the younger a child is, the bigger their head is, in relation to their body?

Tip 2

If a character has their hands by their sides, their elbows hang by their waist, and their hands about halfway between their waist and their knee.

Tip 3

Remember, a person's legs usually take up half of their full height.

A younger child (or a little creature) may be about four heads tall.

A young manga character is around six heads tall.

A grown-up character will be taller, maybe seven or more heads tall.

Here are Makoto, Kimi, Maru and Yamato again. This time you can see all of them.

Makoto is the hero.

Kimi is Makoto's friend.

Maru works for Yamato, who showed him how to change into a boy.

Yamato is always out to make things go wrong for Makoto.

Makoto and Yamato have some similarities. I gave them both a different coloured streak in their hair. I gave Makoto goggles and Yamato glasses.

I thought Kimi would look nice with really long hair. Her hair and dress are cheerful colours because she has a bright and breezy personality.

Maru is really a little monster, so I wanted him to look fierce and quick-moving when he changes into a boy.

Yamato is the oldest, so he is taller. I gave him a big **staff** and a long flowing coat to contrast with Makoto's clothes, which fit more tightly.

Chibi characters

Chibi is a special style of manga drawing which is used when things get a little silly. A chibi character is usually only about three heads high.

I'm chibi style, too!

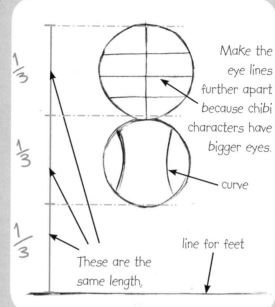

Make the eye lines further apart because chibi characters have bigger eyes.

curve

These are the same length.

line for feet

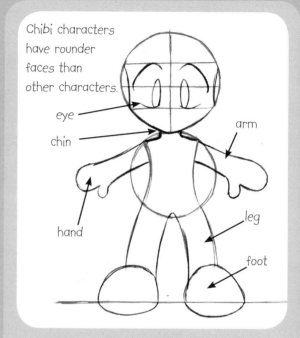

Chibi characters have rounder faces than other characters.

eye

chin

hand

arm

leg

foot

Step 1

- Draw two circles, one on top of the other. The top circle will be the head. Draw guidelines as before.

- The circle underneath will be the body. Draw two curves, one on either side of the body circle, to give it shape, as you can see. Draw a line for where the feet will be.

Step 2

- Next, add shapes for feet on the line you drew, and join them to the body with bendy tubes for legs.

- Use more tubes to make the arms and add simple shapes for hands.

- Give your character a little pointed chin and begin to draw in the eyes as you did for your full-size characters.

Draw the nose and mouth exactly as you did for full-size characters.

Step 3

- Now begin to add details. Finish the eyes, then add a nose and a mouth.

Step 4

- Finish your drawing by going over the lines with ink, then colour it in.

Chibi drawings are easy and fun, so are good things to practise when you are beginning to draw manga.

What to wear?

Now start thinking about what your character is wearing. Clothes can tell you a lot about a person. Even little details show personality. Does he have glasses? Is she wearing jewellery? On these pages you will find some ideas to help you design your character's outfit.

Tip 1

Most clothes can be broken down into simple shapes. One of the most important is the tube. Look at these clothes – they are made from tubes.

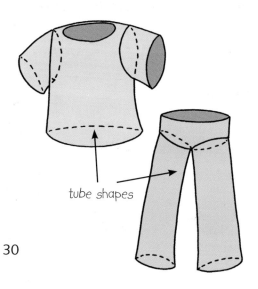

tube shapes

Tip 2

Folds and creases make clothes look real. Folds occur where material stretches or bunches up, for example at the elbow or the knee. Draw lines to show folds.

Folds occur where the elbow is bent.

Zips

Zips are easy. Draw two lines, and in the middle draw a shape like a blunt zigzag for the teeth.

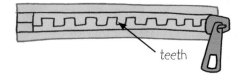

teeth

Belts

Draw a simple belt as a strip with a **rectangle** for a buckle. If you like, you can put in more detail, like this:

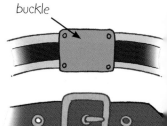

buckle

end of belt

Accessories

Bracelets, necklaces, headbands or glasses make a character look individual.

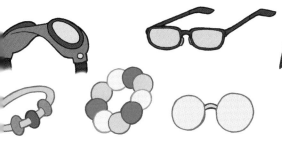

Bows

Bows are easy. Draw a pair of rounded triangles, a small circle and a pair of strips.

Edges

Give clothes a "wavy" edge to make them look as if they are moving. This helps to bring your character to life.

Details

Add details like stitches, buttons and patterns. Think about what kinds of designs your character would like. Would they like flowers or lightning flashes?

Manga masterclass 2: more ideas for faces

More mouths

Here are some more ideas to make your characters special.
Let's see what happens when you draw characters with open mouths.

Tip 1

Draw a shape halfway between the letter O and a sideways D for a character who is talking normally.

Tip 2

Manga mouths are huge when a character is shouting.

Tip 3

A very happy character may give a wide grin.

Little fangs can make a character look strange or wild.

Tip 4

If a character is trying very hard, he might grit his teeth.

Nose tips

Different manga characters have different noses.

Draw a nostril like this.

Tip 1

A small nose, little more than a dot, can look very pretty, especially on young characters.

Tip 2

A bigger, more detailed nose makes a character look older.

Tip 3

Sometimes in very silly or cute drawings, the nose might even be left out altogether!

Out of this world

Manga characters are not always human. There are a lot of strange and fantastic creatures. Why don't you invent your own? Here are a few ideas to get you started.

For eyes like a cat, draw a straight line for the pupil.

Draw ears that are long or pointy.

You could try wings, or even a tail.

What am I supposed to do with this?

Making a manga comic

Once you have some characters, it's time to put them in a manga comic of their own. First, look at how a manga page is put together.

Panels

A page is made up of a series of drawings which tell a story. Most of the time, these drawings are inside boxes called panels. The panels separate one drawing from the next.

Panels are usually rectangles but they can be any shape. In-between the panels there are spaces. These spaces are important because they make the panels stand out and so it is easier to follow the story.

Close ups and long shots

Each panel shows an action by one of the characters, or a moment in the story.

Sometimes, an artist will only show part of a character. This is like a close up in a film, when the camera zooms in to show something important or make it clear what a character is doing. Sometimes, the artist will show the characters in their background from further away. This is like a long shot in a film.

long shot

IT ISN'T FAIR!

AT THIS RATE I'LL NEVER BE STRONG ENOUGH...

HEY...

ARE YOU OKAY?

close up

Words in manga pictures

In a manga comic, there are words as well as pictures.

Speech bubbles

Speech bubbles show what characters are saying to each other.

Hey, can you hear me?

Manga speech bubbles are usually oval, and taller than they are wide. There is a little "tail" pointing to the speaker.

Thought bubbles

A thought bubble shows what characters are thinking.

Hmm ... what to say ...?

Manga thought bubbles are drawn like this.

Sound effects

Manga comics use words to show sound effects.
What might make sounds like these?

Sound effects are not always "real" words.

BANG!

Hsssssss...

SPLAT!

Tkk Tkk Tkk

DRRRRRR!!

Gitaigo

Manga also uses words to describe effects which don't make a noise, like sparkling, smiling or even silence! This is called gitaigo.

SMILE SMILE

Manga characters in action

Manga comics are full of action. It's time to get your characters moving!

Action lines

Use a stick figure to draw different movements, like running or bending. Draw an action line to help you get the movement right. When a character is standing still, the action line is straight. When the character moves, the action line bends or tilts with the movement.

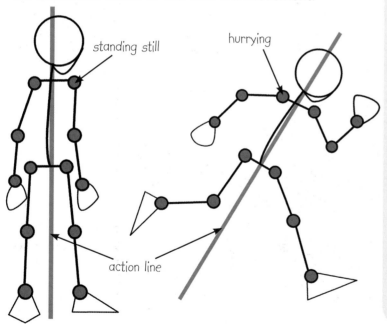

standing still

hurrying

action line

Here are some action lines in action! In these two panels I have left in the action lines so you can see how they have helped me to draw the movements.

Makoto bends down and so does his action line.

Makoto recoils in shock and his action line curves away.

Exaggeration

Make your character's movements even more exciting by **exaggerating** them. This is a running pose.

Now what happens when this pose is exaggerated?

The exaggerated pose looks faster and more exciting.

Movement lines

Another way of showing movement is to add movement lines. These can be shown in two ways.

This movement line follows Makoto's hand.

These movement lines show that Makoto's foot is moving so fast, it looks blurred.

Speed lines

Manga comics use a particular kind of speed lines to make action look more exciting. Speed lines are often drawn to show where a character is coming from, and are usually in the background of the panel.

You can also use speed lines around a character or object to show that something dramatic has happened.

Pattern and colour

Screen tones

Manga artists use screen tones to add shades of grey to black and white manga drawings. Screen tones are sheets of film covered with black dots which are stuck on to the manga drawings. Screen tones can come in cool patterns and they can also be made on the computer. You could even draw similar patterns yourself with a pen.

Using colour

Most manga comics are in black and white, but they often include pictures in colour. Choosing colours for your characters and your panels is fun and can make a big difference to the finished effect. See how different the same picture can look in different colours.

See how different I look!

Bright colours give a lively and exciting effect.

Quieter, duller colours look down-to-earth.

Blues and greys can look cold or sad. If you use dark colours, it can look as if it is night.

Soft pastel colours can look **wistful** or dreamlike.

Manga masterclass 3: special expressions

Manga comes from Japan and it includes features which are different from other comics. Here are some special manga expressions.

Give your drawings a real manga feel.

Breaking a sweat

sweat drop

A teardrop-shaped "sweat drop" shows that a character is upset or embarrassed.

Sneaky

mouth

An especially mischievous character might have a mouth like a sideways 3.

Starry-eyed

A character who is very impressed, or who sees what they really want, may get stars in their eyes!

Over the moon

A big smiley mouth and eyes like upside-down U shapes make a character look very happy.

Burning fury

twitch

A big "twitch" mark around his head, eyes like tilted Ds and no eyebrows, irises or pupils make this character look as if he's about to explode with rage!

Shock horror!

A mouth like this and round eyes with lines underneath and no irises show a character frozen in shock. Squiggly black lines in the background add to the impression of horror.

Strong feelings

A character with sideways V or arrow shapes for eyes will be feeling strongly in some way, either happy, sad or angry.

You said what?!

In a comedy manga story, characters can be so surprised that they fall over!

Manga stories

All manga comics need one very important thing: a good story.

There are many different kinds of manga story. Stories aimed especially at boys are called shonen, and stories aimed mostly at girls are called shoujo, although both can be read by anyone. Both have drama and excitement, but shoujo stories are often about the characters' feelings as well as their actions.

Here are some themes from manga stories:

- children with special powers
- robots or **mecha**
- **ninjas** and martial arts
- people from other worlds
- strange creatures
- school life
- mysteries and secrets.

But manga stories can be about anything. There are exciting manga stories about chess and even baking!

How to write manga stories

The beginning: the problem

All stories have a beginning, middle and end. Once you have some characters the best place to start is with a problem.

If there's no problem, there's no story! It can be a simple problem – the hero is forgetful. One day he forgets his bus money and has to walk home … Or it can be more serious: the heroine's best friend has disappeared and she needs to find him.

I think I've got a problem.

Tip 1

The beginning must grab a reader's attention or they won't want to find out what happens.

A good way to find a problem is to ask "what if" questions for your characters, just as you did when you were creating them.

- What if something dangerous invaded, and only they could stop it?
- What if they were transported to another world, and had to find a way back home?
- What if a new person joined their class, with a mysterious secret?
- What if they were asked to pilot a giant robot?

You must decide what your characters' problem is. The only limit is your imagination!

The middle: the climax

The middle is where the characters are trying to solve their problem and it contains the climax. This is the most exciting part of the story where the characters' success or failure hangs in the balance. Will they work out what to do, or won't they?

Tip 2

It's a good idea to make the characters try to solve the problem in several ways. This keeps the readers guessing.

The end: the resolution

The resolution is the result of what happens in the climax. Did the characters solve their problem? Or did they fail? Either way, in the best stories the characters should have learnt something along the way.

44

Story arcs

A manga story can be short and simple, or it can be longer and more complicated. Longer stories can be made up of groups of smaller, connected stories, and the whole thing is called a story arc.

A story arc has a beginning, middle and end, just like any story, but the characters have to face a number of smaller problems in order to solve the larger one.

For example, a boy and a girl are looking for a golden bracelet, locked away in a hidden chest. They must find a key, then a map and finally travel to a distant land before they can get the bracelet. Each of these stages provides a problem of its own and they will learn different things along the way.

You can make a story arc as long as you like. You can even collect story arcs together to form one big series.

How to make a manga comic

The beginning

Now I'll show how to put characters and story together to make a manga comic. First I need to introduce the characters and their problem: here, Makoto is being bullied by Yamato and Maru when Kimi arrives.

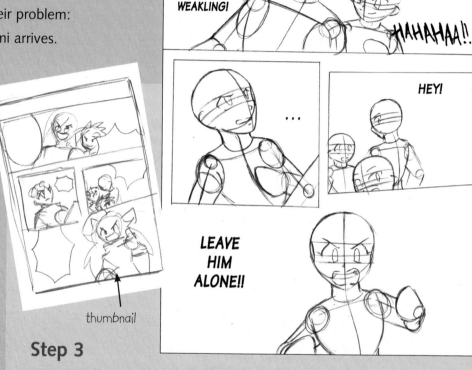

Step 1

I've chosen to do four drawings on the first page:

- Yamato and Maru bully Makoto.
- Makoto feels bad.
- Someone is coming.
- It's Makoto's friend Kimi.

Don't try to put too much on each page!

Step 2

Next, work out where the panels should go. Draw a small, rough plan. This is called a thumbnail.

Remember to leave gaps between the panels.

thumbnail

Step 3

Now neatly draw your thumbnail so it fills a whole page. Next, draw your characters in pencil in the panels. Write out what they are saying and leave spaces for the speech bubbles. Make sure everything fits before adding too many details, in case you need to make changes.

Step 4

Draw speech bubbles around the words and finish the pencil drawings. Add a background, if you like, to show where your story is happening.

Step 5

Go over the lines in ink. Do the panel boxes, speech bubbles and sound effects first. When the ink is dry, rub out the pencil lines. Finish off the page by adding details and patterns with a thin pen to make it look more interesting.

The middle and the climax

OH NO! QUICK, HE'S GOING TO TRANSFORM!

HAHAHAHA!!

OH YEAH!?

YOU'LL NEVER CATCH ME NOW!

WE'LL SEE ABOUT THAT!!

The panels have slanted edges. This shows that things are getting tense.

Use really exaggerated poses and plenty of speed lines to make the action move.

Now Kimi and Makoto have to stop Yamato and Maru bullying them. How could they do this? There are lots of different adventures they could have, but I've suggested what might happen in the middle of the story. Here are two pages from the climax.

Story: Yamato has sent Maru to steal Makoto's special bracelet. Kimi and Makoto are chasing Maru to get the bracelet back. Just as they are about to catch him, Maru transforms into his chibi-shape.

Story continued: At last Kimi manages to get the bracelet back from Maru. Then Yamato appears but Makoto finds the courage to stand up to Yamato and Maru. As he does so, Makoto finds he has special powers.

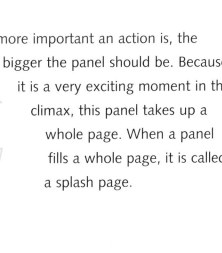

The more important an action is, the bigger the panel should be. Because it is a very exciting moment in the climax, this panel takes up a whole page. When a panel fills a whole page, it is called a splash page.

If someone is shouting, the speech bubble is pointy and the words are jagged.

The end: resolution

When the problem is solved, it's time to end the story. In a good story, each challenge should change the characters in some way. When we leave them, much later in the story, Kimi has shown herself to be a true and brave friend. Makoto has found inner strength and confidence and Yamato has learnt that there is more to life than being powerful. The two of them part ways as friendly rivals.

But the end of this story is not the end of the characters. Perhaps they will have more adventures in new stories.

More manga ideas

The more manga you read, the more ideas you will get for new stories and characters. You'll find manga books in your library and in bookshops.

It's especially fun to read manga with your friends, because you can swap comics and talk about your favourite characters. Now you have learnt more about drawing manga characters, try making your own comics. You could create stories for each other to draw and put your stories together into a collection.

See you next time! Bye!

Glossary

energetic   lively, full of energy

exaggerating   deliberately making something more extreme

expressions   changes in a person's face which reflect their feelings

features   (1) parts of the face, like the eyes and nose

            (2) things that are special about an idea, object or person

gleeful   joyful and excited

iris   the coloured ring in a person's eye

mecha   robot characters that are often found in manga comics

mischievous   naughty, trouble-making

ninjas   masked warriors trained in martial arts

proportions   the way in which different things compare to each other in size – in this case, parts of the body

pupil   the dark circle in the middle of a person's eye

rectangle   a stretched square, where two of the facing sides are longer

sphere   a shape like a ball

staff   a long stick, used as a walking stick, which can also be a symbol of power

stylised   drawn in a way that is different from real life, but very recognisable

underdog   someone who is weaker than others, and not expected to do well

wistful   thoughtful and a bit sad

Index

A mind map of manga

comics

mainly black and white
but some colour

features

often published in
big books weekly

special effects

characters

style

What is manga?

gitaigo

speed lines

movement lines

screen tones

speech bubbles

thought bubbles

all kinds:

powerful children

people from other worlds

people with special powers

monsters

underdogs

big eyes

wild hair

larger heads

chibi style

action-filled plots

from Japan

popular everywhere

especially:

Japan
Australia
Europe
USA

subjects

readers

adults
children
girls
boys
all nationalities

Japanese comics read right to left.

includes Japanese words:

mangaka
anime
shoujo
shonen
mecha
ninja
gitaigo
chibi

fact

fiction:

real life
fantasy
science fiction
drama
school life
sports
animals
shonen
shoujo

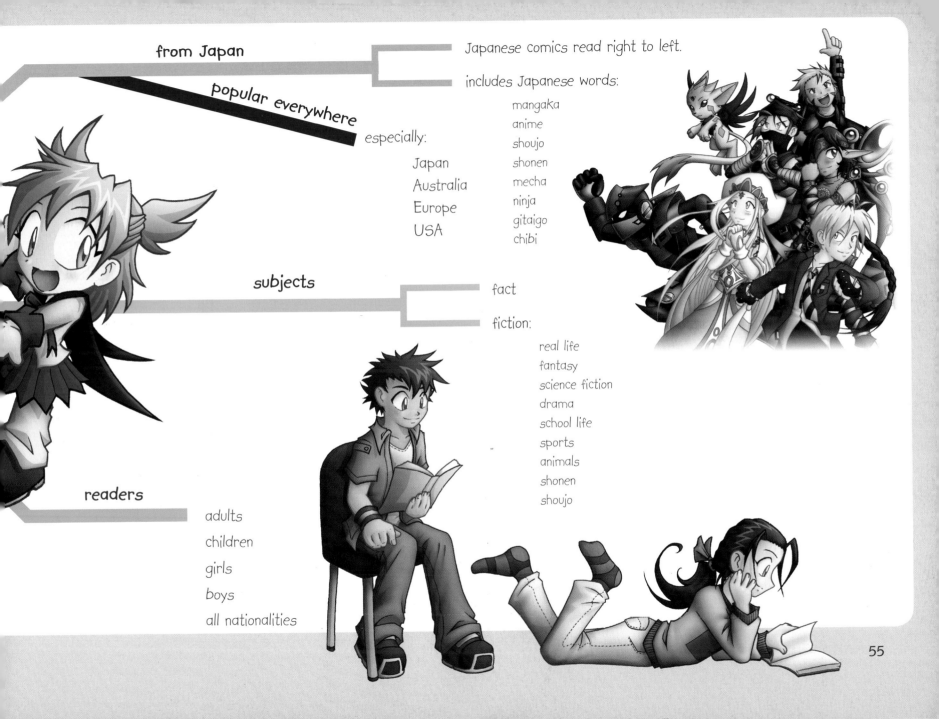

Ideas for reading

Written by Clare Dowdall, PhD
Lecturer and Primary Literacy Consultant

Reading objectives:
- retrieve, record and present information from non-fiction
- identify how language, structure and presentation contribute to meaning
- provide reasoned justifications for their views
- explain and discuss their understanding of what they have read, including through formal presentations

Spoken language objectives:
- give well-structured descriptions, explanations and narratives for different purposes
- ask relevant questions to extend their understanding and knowledge
- maintain attention and participate actively in collaborative conversations

Curriculum links: Art and Design

Interest words: anime, chibi, gitaigo, mangaka, mecha, ninjas

Resources: manga and other comics, anime cartoons

Build a context for reading

This book can be read over two or more reading sessions.

- Read the front and back covers together. Discuss what is known about manga comics and characters (e.g. where does manga originate?).
- Ask children to share any previous experiences of reading manga comics and watching manga cartoons/playing games with manga characters.

- Look carefully at the images on the covers. List some of the features that manga characters have (e.g. huge, expressive eyes, funky hair). Discuss the contribution that these illustrations might make to a manga story.

Understand and apply reading strategies

- Prior to reading *What is manga?*, in pairs, ask children to list the questions that they still have about manga (e.g. Who reads manga? How long has manga existed?).

- Model how to find answers to these questions, using the contents and index.

- Read to p8 as a group. Discuss the range of techniques that the author has used to interest and inform the reader (e.g. the use of questions as headings, real examples, bullet points).

- Ask children to read pp8–16. Give them time to follow the instructions and to draw their own manga head.

Develop reading and language comprehension

- As a group, discuss and evaluate how helpful the instructions for drawing a manga head were. Help children make reference to the text to justify their arguments.

- Return to the contents. In pairs, ask children to choose and read another chapter that interests them, looking for three key ideas.